Botts's Dots
Not just a bump in the road

story by Roz Silva
Art by Lisa Mulvaney Gillespie

Text copyright © 2018 Roz Silva
Illustrations copyright © 2018 Lisa Mulvaney Gillespie
All rights reserved

No part of this book may be used or reproduced in any manner without written permission from the publisher, except brief excerpts used in the context of a review.

Set in Stone Serif (Stone Type Foundry) and Luna (Amanda Leeson)

Printed and bound in USA

Dayton Publishing LLC
Solana Beach, CA 92075
858-775-3629
publisher@daytonpublishing.com
www.daytonpublishing.com

ISBN-13: 978-1-7325265-0-1

To Italia and Lily Silva and all the rides we shared on the freeways between Los Angeles and San Diego, which inspired this book.
— Roz Silva

To the Mulvaneys and Gillespies
— L.M.G.

---

*This book would not have been possible without the help of librarians and others at the California Department of Transportation, who answered our questions and found the reference materials we requested in the archives.
Thank you so much, Caltrans.*

Dr. Elbert Dysart Botts was a hero of the modern era. As an engineer working at a division of California's Department of Public Works that was later called Caltrans, he developed the pavement markers known as **Botts Dots.**

"We have to make the roads more safe —
  there has to be a way,"
  Elbert Botts said to himself
  one wet and rainy day.

"It's hard to see the freeway lines whenever we have rain,

and workers have to risk their lives when they repaint a lane."

So Dr. Botts, there in his lab, developed dome-like dots — those small reflective markers, those little disc-like spots.

The dots took time to figure out,
to get them made just so.

But how to stick them to the road? Botts simply didn't know.

At first he thought of using nails,
but that would never do.
The nails and dots could separate
and pop a tire or two!

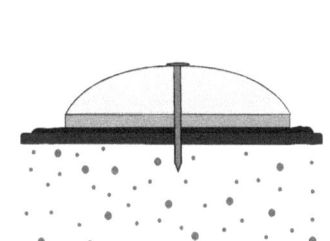
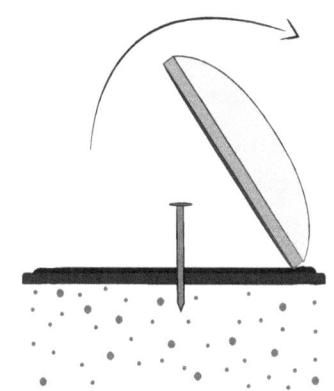
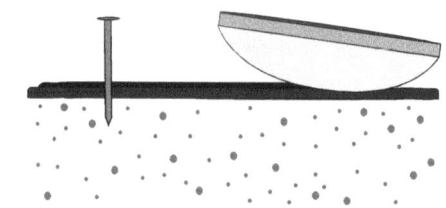

POP!!!!!

Dr. Botts passed away
before his task was through.
His research stopped, the dots on hold
— till finally, a glue!

His notes were found and
Botts's partners finished his design —
a way to stick them to the road
and keep them in a line.

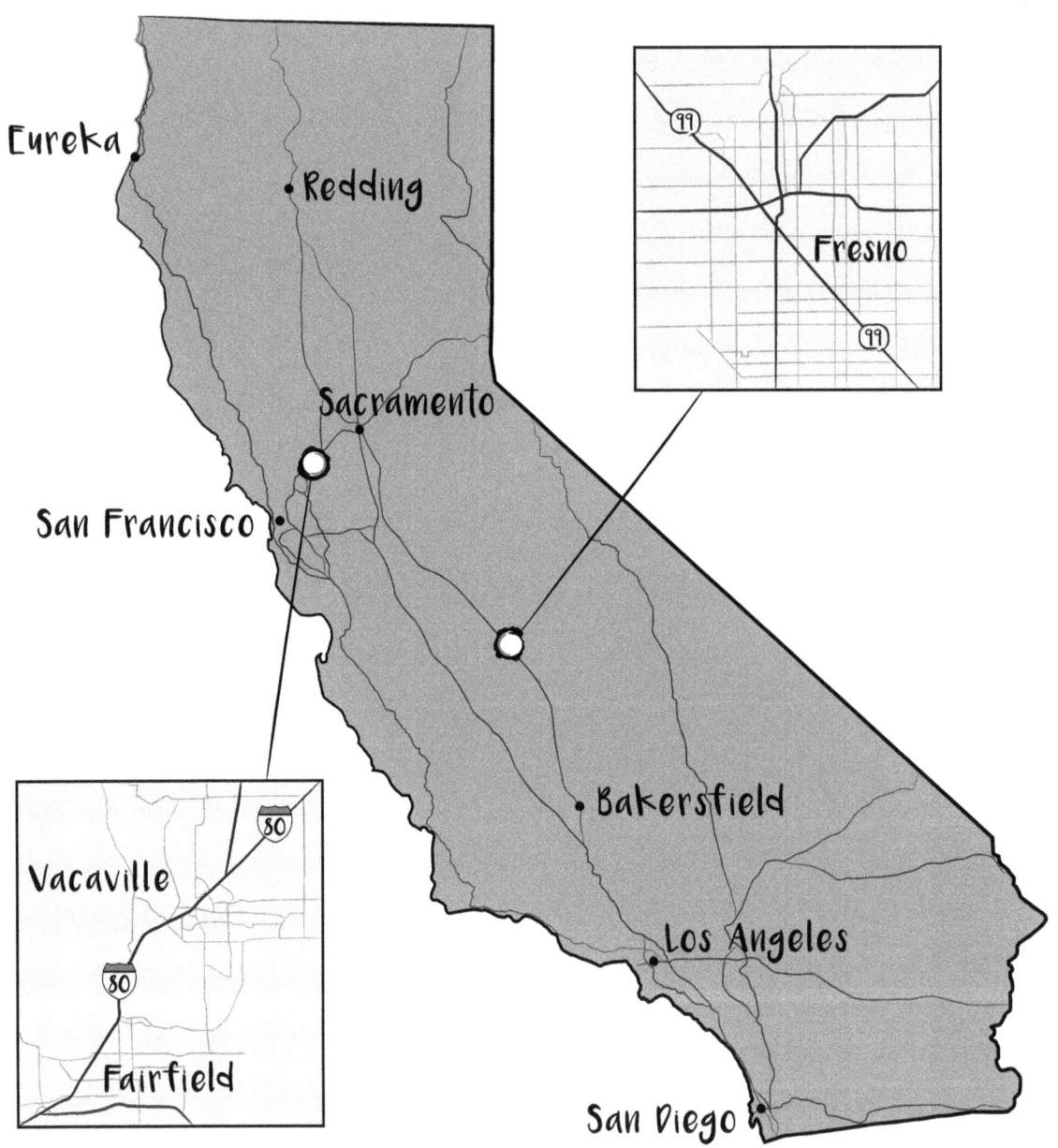

In 1966 the dots were finally installed on California freeways that were being overhauled.

Soon after, there were rows of dots,
lined up between reflectors,
on most of California's roadways,
freeways and connectors.

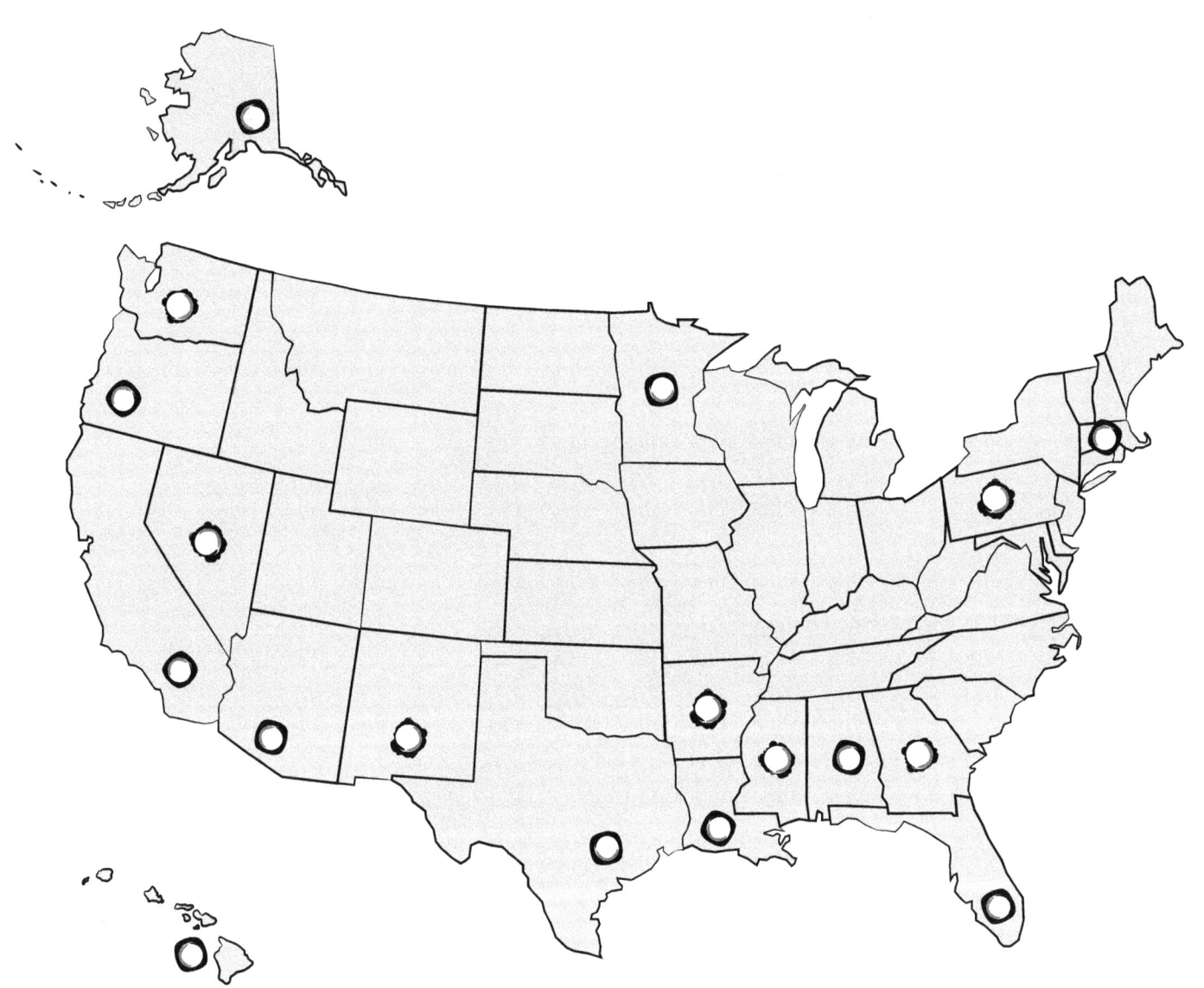

Year by year more states and countries
put the dots to use,
anywhere that snow-plow blades
wouldn't pry them loose.

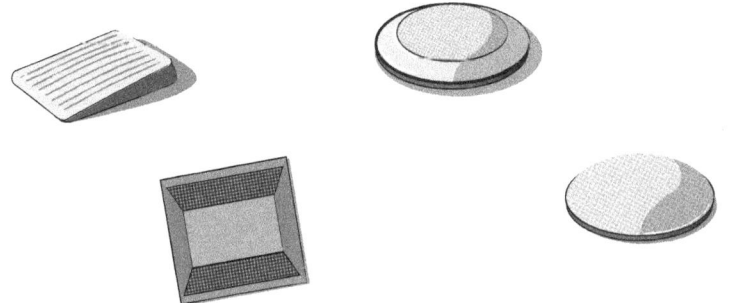

Some places they're called "turtles."
Some people call them "bumps."
Others call them "buttons"
— those cookie-looking lumps.

Whatever you might call them,
the dots sure saved the day —
bright markers splitting highway lanes
and showing us the way.

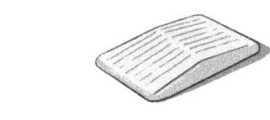

Though Botts had worked for many years
perfecting his invention,
that thump they make when they're run over
wasn't his intention.

The "rumble" that you hear, though,
is every driver's gift —
because it gives a warning
if your car begins to "drift."

For more than 50 years the dots
have saved so many lives,
by waking drivers "nodding off"
on long and tiring drives.

"I must have been falling asleep. The vibration from going over the dots woke me up. My heart was racing."

"The kids were squabbling in the back seat. I took my eyes off the road just for a second to check on them. The dots did their job. We were lucky."

"Botts Dots help me stay in my lane, especially on those slow, foggy commutes."

When Dr. Botts invented dots,
the roads were lightly traveled.
But much more use by many cars
can turn the dots to gravel.

And now, we hear, the use of dots
is coming to an end,
as better stripe technology
becomes the newest trend.

More durable than dots, the stripes
are simpler to maintain.
And newer cars can "see" the stripes
to stay within their lane.

Dr. Botts's dots
never brought him wealth or fame.
But the work he did for Caltrans
will always bear his name.

Elbert Dysart Botts and His Dots: A Timeline

January 2, 1893 Born in Lancaster, Missouri, to Benjamin Botts, a farmer from Indiana, and his wife, Emily Ann Mitchell Botts

1918 Graduated from Albany College in Oregon

1923 Married Iris Elizabeth Kingsley in Cook County, Illinois

1924 Awarded a Ph.D in Chemistry by University of Wisconsin

1924 Employed as Chief Chemist for American Marine Paint Company in San Francisco

1926 Lost his wife, Iris, who died in childbirth

1928–1944 Served as a Professor of Chemistry at San Jose State College, San Jose, California

1929 Married Gretchen Kroncke of Madison, Wisconsin

1942 Served as technical adviser to the Smaller War Plants Corporation and U. S. Department of Commerce in Los Angeles during World War II

1950 Began working at California Department of Transportation in the Materials and Research Department as Senior Chemical Testing Engineer

1953 Oversaw research that led to the development of Botts Dots, raised pavement markers

1960 Retired from the California Department of Public Works, Division of Highways (later called Caltrans)

April 10, 1962 Died in Sutter General Hospital in Sacramento, California, after a long illness

1965–'66 Pattern of four Botts Dots between reflectors installed on two California freeways

1997 More than 25 million Botts Dots in use on California freeways alone

2017 Botts Dots no longer being installed in California

Moving forward — Millions of the Dots are still in service, but as freeways are resurfaced, the Dots are often removed and replaced with new striping technology.

About the Author

Roz Silva, a writer, editor and publicist, is a former educator of her own four children as well as those in the Chula Vista Elementary School district, where she has served as a substitute teacher for the past 20 years. She has been traversing the California freeways for 15 years in order to see her two granddaughters, Italia and Lily, regretfully leaving behind two adopted mixed terriers, Tito and Franco. She lives in Chula Vista, California, with her husband, Fred. Her previous books include ***Three Tales, Four Dogs*** and ***Playmates for Puppies,*** both published by Dayton Publishing.

About the Illustrator

Lisa Mulvaney Gillespie began her career as a 3D Artist in video games. Since that time, she has channeled her love for digital art into illustration and graphic design. Lisa completed coursework at Pratt Institute and earned a B.A. in Visual Arts from the University of California, San Diego. She lives in San Diego with her husband, James, son, Anton, two cats, and a chihuahua-terrier mix named Leo Samuels. *Botts's Dots* is her first book for children.

www.ingramcontent.com/pod-product-compliance
Lightning Source LLC
Chambersburg PA
CBHW061141070526
44584CB00033B/4391